Complete Student K

Business English

TWELFTH EDITION

Mary Ellen Guffey

Carolyn M. Seefer

CENGAGE
Learning·

Australia • Brazil • Mexico • Singapore • United Kingdom • United States

For product information and technology assistance, contact us at **Cengage Learning Customer & Sales Support, 1-800-354-9706**.

For permission to use material from this text or product, submit all requests online at **www.cengage.com/permissions** Further permissions questions can be emailed to **permissionrequest@cengage.com**.

ISBN: 978-1-305-64154-9

Cengage Learning
20 Channel Center Street
Boston, MA 02210
USA

Cengage Learning is a leading provider of customized learning solutions with office locations around the globe, including Singapore, the United Kingdom, Australia, Mexico, Brazil, and Japan. Locate your local office at: **www.cengage.com/global**.

Cengage Learning products are represented in Canada by Nelson Education, Ltd.

To learn more about Cengage Learning Solutions, visit **www.cengage.com**.

Purchase any of our products at your local college store or at our preferred online store **www.cengagebrain.com**.

Printed in the United States of America
Print Number: 01   Print Year: 2015

Table of Contents

Answers to Reinforcement Exercises

Chapter 1
A. **Chapter 1 Preview.**

1.	a	6.	c
2.	c	7.	d
3.	d	8.	b
4.	b	9.	b
5.	a	10.	b

B. **Recognizing Parts of Speech.**

11.	c	16.	c
12.	a	17.	d
13,	d	18.	d
14.	b	19.	a
15.	d	20.	b

C. **Parts of Speech.**

21.	c	26.	c
22.	a	27.	a
23.	b	28.	d
24.	b	29.	a
25.	c	30.	b

D. **Writing Exercise: Parts of Speech.**
31. All parties signed the contract.
32. Did you contract much debt during the recession?
33. We hired a contract worker to upgrade our network.
34. The father-daughter dance was a big hit.
35. Many people dance to exercise and to relieve stress.
36. A new dance club opened near our office.
37. They drove across the desert on the way to the conference.
38. She is afraid her teammates will desert her.
39. Would you like to be stranded on a desert island?
40. The hostess served a decadent dessert after dinner.

E. **Parts of Speech.**

41.	adjective (article)	48.	verb
42.	adjective	49.	adverb
43.	noun	50.	verb
44.	verb	51.	interjection
45.	noun	52.	pronoun
46.	conjunction	53.	adverb
47.	pronoun	54.	verb
55.	adjective	58.	adjective
56.	noun	59.	adjective
57.	preposition	60.	noun

F.   Verbs.

61. b (action)
62. a (action)
63. b (linking)
64. c (linking)
65. b (action)

66. b (action)
67. b (linking)
68. a (linking)
69. b (action)
70. a (linking)

G.   Writing Exercise. Parts of Speech.

Answers will vary.

It is important to understand how the parts of speech work so that I can talk about them in this course. On the job it is important to know the parts of speech so that when I look up words in a dictionary, I understand how they may function in sentences. Knowing the parts of speech will also help me punctuate correctly.

Nouns name persons, places, things, qualities, feelings, concepts, activities, and measures. They are important because they are the subjects of sentences and the objects of verbs. Verbs show the action in a sentence and can also be used to link words to the subject or to rename the subject. Writers often say that verbs are more important than nouns because they evoke feelings.

H.   FAQs About Business English Review.

71. b
72. c
73. b
74. b
75. a

76. c
77. d
78. a
79. b
80. a

Chapter 2

A.   Chapter 2 Preview.

1. T
2. F
3. T
4. T
5. F

6. T
7. F
8. F
9. T
10. T

B.   Sentence Elements.

11. a
12. b
13. b
14. a
15. d

16. b
17. d
18. b
19. b
20. b

C. Phrases and Clauses.

21.	D	26.	D
22.	I	27.	I
23.	I	28.	P
24.	D	29.	D
25.	P	30.	P

D. Sentence Varieties.

31.	simple	36.	simple
32.	compound	37.	complex
33.	simple	38.	simple
34.	compound	39.	complex
35.	complex	40.	simple

E. Writing Exercise. Sentence Patterns.

Answers will vary.

41.	succeeded.	54.	accountant.
42.	is moving.	55.	she.
43.	delegate.	56.	he *or* Ms. Jones.
44.	have increased.	57.	enjoyable.
45.	voted.	58.	chic.
46.	is closing.	59.	friendly.
47.	contract.	60.	longer.
48.	packages.	61.	you
49.	it.	62.	office
50.	laws.	63.	applicants
51.	dividends.	64.	were
52.	party.	65.	are
53.	Katharine.	66.	lives

F. Sentence Types.

67.	c	72.	d
68.	a	73.	c
69.	d	74.	b
70.	b	75.	a
71.	a	76.	b

G. Sentence Faults.

77.	a	82.	d
78.	c	83.	b
79.	a	84.	d
80.	b	85.	c
81.	a	86.	a

H.   Writing Exercise. Sentence Fragments.

Answers will vary.

87.   Because I want to pursue a career in health care management, I am interested in your degree program.

88.   We are seeking a health care manager who has not only good communication skills but also medical expertise.

89.   During job interviews candidates must provide details about their accomplishments, which is why they should rehearse answers to expected questions.

90.   Although an interviewer will typically start with general questions about your background, be careful to respond with a brief history.

I.   Writing Exercise. Sentence Varieties, Patterns, and Types.

Solutions will vary.

J.   FAQs About Business English Review.

91.	c	96.	a
92.	a	97.	b
93.	a	98.	b
94.	b	99.	a
95.	b	100.	c

Chapter 3

Level 1

A.   Level 1 Preview.

1.	c	6.	c
2.	c	7.	b
3.	b	8.	a
4.	b	9.	a
5.	a	10.	c

B.   Plural Nouns.

11.	a	21.	b
12.	b	22.	c
13.	a	23.	b
14.	b	24.	b
15.	b	25.	a
16.	a	26.	b
17.	c	27.	a
18.	b	28.	c
19.	c	29.	b
20.	a	30.	a

C. Writing Exercise. Plural Nouns.

31.	PhDs	41.	blitzes
32.	lice	42.	depts.
33.	speeches	43.	geese
34.	Nos.	44.	biases
35.	franchises	45.	A's
36.	quotas	46.	Cs
37.	subsidiaries	47.	governors-elect
38.	feet	48.	women
39.	balances of trade	49.	logos
40.	Gomezes	50.	oxen

D. Writing Exercise, Plural Nouns.

Answers will vary.

51. Minneapolis has approved three new businesses for the area along the Mississippi River.
52. We have a large selection of clothing and accessories for children.
53. Have the Alvarezes been invited?
54. Many standbys (not *standbies*) waited to get on the crowded flight.
55. Do you know the ins and outs of the hospitality industry?
56. She handles the portfolios for several large clients.
57. Many ordinary heroes live among us.
58. The defense plans to call five witnesses to the stand.
59. We drove through several valleys on our way to Hana.
60. Two bailiffs will escort the defendant into the courtroom.

Level 2

A. Level 2 Preview.

61.	a	66.	b
62.	c	67.	b
63.	c	68.	c
64.	a	69.	b
65.	c	70.	a

B. Writing Exercise. Possessive Nouns.

71.	the four CPAs' credentials	76.	the company's Twitter feed
72.	the students' LinkedIn accounts	77.	the two companies' merger
73.	the student's college application	78.	competitors' prices
74.	the sister-in-law's luncheon	79.	several doctor's offices
75.	customers' addresses	80.	a doctor's appointment calendar

C. Plural and Possessive Nouns.

81. citizens'
82. viruses
83. witness's
84. Passengers'
85. employees
86. organizations'
87. companies
88. companies'
89. skills
90. individual's

91. subscribers
92. States
93. Graphics
94. staff's
95. SEC's
96. electronics
97. NBC's
98. NAFTA's
99. Norris's
100. Inc.'s

D. Writing Exercise. Possessive Nouns.

101. The support of John F. Kennedy's father was instrumental to the U.S. president's political success.
102. The hourly fee of my sister's lawyer is high.
103. The success of John Grisham's latest book has been overwhelming.
104. The laptop of the engineer's assistant held all the necessary equations.
105. The motor home of my supervisor's friend is always parked in the company lot.

Level 3

A. Level 3 Preview.

106. a
107. b
108. a
109. b
110. b

111. a
112. b
113. b
114. c
115. b

B. Plural Nouns.

116. b
117. c
118. a
119. a
120. b

121. a
122. c
123. a
124. c
125. a

C. Plural and Possessive Nouns.

126. Robert
127. company's
128. buyers'
129. Meaghan's
130. week's

131. master's
132. dollar's
133. years'
134. Thanks
135. headquarters

D.   **Review of Plural and Possessive Nouns.**

136. avionics
137. ATMs
138. A's
139. armies
140. stimuli
141. Ruizes
142. employees
143. pros
144. e-portfolios
145. brothers-in-law

146. bachelor's
147. boss's
148. guests'
149. CPAs
150. diagnoses
151. cents'
152. credentials
153. waitress's
154. Charlie's

E.   **Writing Exercise. Noun Possessives.**

Answers will vary.
155. Susan's and Gary's test results were almost identical.
156. Susan and Gary's son started college this year.
157. The contractor's bid was too high.
158. Some of Congress's latest laws may not withstand judicial review.
159. All customer's comments and suggestions are taken seriously.
160. Her mother-in-law's home was within walking distance.

F.   **FAQs About Business English Review.**

161. a
162. b
163. b
164. c
165. a

166. c
167. a
168. a
169. b
170. a

Chapter 4
Level 1
A.   **Level 1 Preview.**

1. him
2. your
3. its
4. I
5. us

6. she
7. her and me
8. me
9. her
10. he

B.   **Subjective and Objective Pronouns.**

11. a
12. c
13. a
14. b
15. c

16. c
17. a
18. b
19. a
20. c

C.   Personal Pronouns.

21.	me	31.	I
22.	her	32.	me
23.	me	33.	us
24.	I	34.	she
25.	I	35.	me
26.	him	36.	him and her
27.	himself	37.	her
28.	we	38.	they
29.	they	39.	him
30.	him	40.	he

D.   Possessive Pronouns and Contractions.

41.	yours	46.	You're
42.	its	47.	theirs
43.	hers	48.	It's
44.	There's	49.	Your
45.	its	50.	Ours

E.   Review of Personal Pronouns.

51.	me	61.	me
52.	she	62.	theirs
53.	he	63.	hers
54.	her	64.	she
55.	me	65.	its
56.	its	66.	it's
57.	he	67.	us
58.	we	68.	You're
59.	I	69.	she
60.	her	70.	yours

F.   Writing Exercise. Personal Pronouns.

Answers will vary.

71.   The two consultants, Lisa and he, visited our main office this past Friday.
72.   Except for Yumiko and me, everyone has gone home.
73.   The manager expected Jeff and me to work late whenever necessary.
74.   The building and its contents were destroyed by fire.
75.   Ours is the only office without its own parking spaces.

Level 2

A.   Level 2 Preview.

76.	b	81.	a
77.	b	82.	b
78.	a	83.	b
79.	a	84.	b
80.	c	85.	a

B.   Pronoun–Antecedent Agreement.

86.	c	96.	b
87.	c	97.	b
88.	b	98.	b
89.	a	99.	a
90.	b	100.	a
91.	b	101.	a
92.	a	102.	b
93.	c	103.	b
94.	a	104.	b
95.	d	105.	a

C.   Writing Exercise. Gender Agreement.

Answers will vary.

106. a. All arriving passengers must have their luggage searched by customs officials.
     b. Every arriving passenger must have all luggage searched by customs officials.
     c. Every arriving passenger must have his or her luggage searched by customs officials.
107. a. Be sure that all new employees have received their orientation packets.
     b. Be sure that each new employee has received an orientation packet.
     c. Be sure that each new employee has received his or her orientation packet.
108. a. Doctors must submit their insurance paperwork on time.
     b. A doctor must submit all insurance paperwork on time.
     c. A doctor must submit his or her insurance paperwork on time.

D.   Writing exercise. Clear Pronoun Reference.

Answers will vary.

109. The article reported that Facebook had acquired WhatsApp for $19 billion and that Facebook planned to use WhatsApp communication technology to dominate the smartphone messaging market.
110. Management makes customers wear coats and ties in that restaurant.
111. Mr. Winterstein told Mr. Petrino that Mr. Petrino needs to take a vaction.
112. Recruiters like to see job objectives on résumés; however, such objectives may restrict job candidates' chances.
113. Ms. Hartman talked with Lisbeth about Lisbeth's telecommuting request, but Ms. Hartman needed more information.

Level 3
A.   Level 3 Preview.

114.	Whom	119.	whom
115.	who	120.	Who
116.	who	121.	who
117.	whoever	122.	who's
118.	whom	123.	Whose

B. *Who/Whoever* and *Whom/Whomever*.

124. who	134. who
125. whoever	135. who
126. who	136. whoever
127. who	137. whom
128. Whom	138. whom
129. whom	139. who
130. whoever	140. whom
131. whom	141. whom
132. who	142. who
133. whomever	143. who

C. *Whose/Who's*.

144. Who's	149. whose
145. Whose	150. who's
146. Who's	151. whose
147. Who's	152. Whose
148. Who's	153. Who's

D.   Review. Pronouns.

154. its	164. its
155. its	165. her
156. their	166. Who's
157. his or her	167. its
158. its	168. who
159. its	169. whoever
160. whom	170. its
161. whoever	171. his or her
162. his	172. their
163. Whom	173. whose

E.   FAQs About Business English Review.

174. a	179. b
175. b	180. b
176. a	181. b
177. b	182. b
178. c	183. c

Chapter 5
Level 1
A. Level 1 Preview.

1. a	6. b
2. b	7. b
3. a	8. b
4. a	9. b
5. a	10. a

B.   Active and Passive Voice.

11. a	16. a
12. a	17. a
13. b	18. b
14. b	19. a
15. b	20. b

C.   Writing Exercise. Active and Passive Voice.

21. The Food and Drug Administration does not currently evaluate diet pills and weight-loss supplements for safety.
22. Toyota designed a car with solar panels that will power the air-conditioning system.
23. Filipinos send approximately one billion text messages every day.
24. Apple considered sapphire scratch-resistant display screens for its iPhones.
25. Insurance companies offer doctors cash rewards for prescribing generic drugs.
26. In the United States, Google is testing a self-driving car with neither a steering wheel nor pedals.
27. You must carefully calculate net income before taxes when you fill out your tax return.
28. Investigators cautiously reviewed the documents during the audit.
29. The author detected only a few of the many errors and change during the first proofreading.
30. AT&T constructed a cell phone tower in their neighborhood.

D.   Writing Exercise. Primary Tenses.

31. worried, worries, will worry	36. covered, covers, will cover
32. opened, opens, will open	37. planned, plans, will plan
33. copied, copies, will copy	38. invested, invests, will invest
34. carried, carries, will carry	39. selected, select, will select
35. tried, tries, will try	40. sampled, sample, will sample

Level 2
A. Level 2 Preview.

41. a	46. b
42. b	47. a
43. a	48. b
44. b	49. b
45. b	50. a

B.   Gerunds and Infinitives.

51. b	56. b
52. b	57. a
53. a	58. a
54. b	59. b
55. b	60. b

C.   Writing Exercise. Misplaces Verbal Modifiers.
Answers will vary.
61.   After breaking into the building, the burglars set off an alarm heard by the police.
62.   To be binding, every contract must be supported by a consideration.
63.   Scattered all over my desk, the many files for our project surprised my manager.
64.   Selected as Employee of the Year, Cecile Chang was presented an award by the CEO.
65.   Driving to the sales meeting, he turned the radio to NPR.
66.   Here are some tips from our insurance company for protecting your identity.
67.   An investor said that someone stole a coin collection valued at $50,000 from a safe in his home office.
68.   Walking hand in hand from the helicopter, William and Kate left Buckingham Palace, where they stayed the night.
69.   Dave found his wallet lying under the front seat of his car.
70.   From a helicopter, geologists inspected the site where the builders broke free.

D.   Subjunctive Mood.

71.	b	76.	a
72.	b	77.	a
73.	c	78.	b
74.	b	79.	b
75.	a	80.	a

Level 3
A.   Level 3 Preview.

81.	c	86.	b
82.	b	87.	b
83.	b	88.	b
84.	b	89.	a
85.	a	90.	c

B.   Irregular Verbs.

91.	b	101.	a
92.	c	102.	b
93.	b	103.	a
94.	b	104.	c
95.	a	105.	a
96.	b	106.	b
97.	b	107.	a
98.	a	108.	b
99.	b	109.	b
100.	c	110.	b

C. *Lie–Lay*

111. b	116. b
112. b	117. a
113. a	118. a
114. a	119. b
115. b	120. a

D. *Sit–Set; Rise–Raise*

121. a	126. a
122. a	127. a
123. a	128. b
124. b	129. a
125. b	130. a

E.   Writing Exercise. Irregular Verbs.
Answers will vary.
131. Funds were drawn mysteriously from her personal account.
132. I lent a colleague $10 for lunch.
133. Connor has sung in the church choir for several years.
134. Sheila caught the flu from her son.
135. This whole issue has been blown out of proportion.
136. Several pages were torn from the law book.
137. She drank iced tea with her lunch.
138. The bad debt was forgiven.
139. He is driven to earn good grades.
140. Several questions arose during the meeting.

F.   FAQs About Business English Review.

141. b	146. a
142. b	147. a
143. a	148. a
144. b	149. b
145. a	150. b

Chapter 6
Level 1
A.   Level 1 Preview.

1. b	6. b
2. a	7. b
3. b	8. a
4. b	9. a
5. a	10. a

B. Identifying Subjects.

11.	a	16.	b
12.	c	17.	a
13.	a	18.	c
14.	c	19.	a
15.	a	20.	c

C. Subject–Verb Agreement.
21. subject: array; ~~of prices and specifications for these tablets~~; a
22. subject: variety; ~~of products made from recyclable materials~~; a
23. subject: use; ~~of smartphones and tablets~~; a
24. subject: degree; ~~from an accredited institution~~; years; ~~of experience~~; b
25. subject: Everyone; ~~except temporary workers employed during the last year~~; a
26. subject: wingspan; ~~on each of Boeing's latest passenger planes~~; a
27. subject: cooperatives; ~~except the Lemon Growing Exchange~~; b
28. subject: one; ~~of the major automobile manufacturers~~; a
29. subject: entrepreneurs; ~~such as Donald Trump~~; b
30. subject: topic; ~~along with benefits and vacation time~~; a

D. Subject–Verb Agreement.

31.	b	41.	a
32.	a	42.	b
33.	a	43.	a
34.	a	44.	b
35.	a	45.	a
36.	b	46.	a
37.	b	47.	a
38.	a	48.	a
39.	a	49.	a
40.	b	50.	a

Level 2
A. Level 2 Preview.

51.	a	56.	a
52.	a	57.	a
53.	a	58.	a
54.	b	59.	a
55.	a	60.	b

B.   Subject–Verb Agreement.

61.	b	71.	a
62.	a	72.	a
63.	b	73.	b
64.	a	74.	b
65.	b	75.	a
66.	a	76.	b
67.	a	77.	a
68.	b	78.	a
69.	a	79.	b
70.	a	80.	a

C.   Writing Exercise. Subject–Verb Agreement.

81.   opposed to additional budget cuts.
82.   raising their hands to vote on the issue.
83.   recently voted to restrict spending.
84.   acceptable to the committee.
85.   that meetings should be scheduled to avoid conflicts.
86.   to be rewritten.
87.   using a cell phone.
88.   responsible for locking up.
89.   responsible for locking up.
90.   inspiring.

Level 3
A.   Level 3 Preview.

91.	a	96.	a
92.	b	97.	b
93.	a	98.	a
94.	a	99.	a
95.	b	100.	a

B.   Subject–Verb Agreement.

101.	b	111.	b
102.	b	112.	a
103.	b	113.	a
104.	a	114.	b
105.	a	115.	a
106.	b	116.	b
107.	a	117.	a
108.	a	118.	a
109.	b	119.	b
110.	a	120.	a

C. Writing Exercise. Subject–Verb Agreement.
Answers will vary.
121. Significant advantages for college graduates are recent training and technology skills.
122. The best parts of my job are greeting and interacting with customers.
123. Important factors in McDonald's sales slump are fast-casual restaurants and gourmet-burger eateries such as Five Guys and Chipotle.
124. The primary reasons for his wealth are wise stock and other investment choices.
125. The most important traits I have to offer an employer are energy and enthusiasm.

D. Review. Subject–Verb Agreement.

126. has		136. is
127. There are		137. seems
128. is		138. are
129. cause		139. is
130. Were		140. surrounds
131. has		141. has
132. were		142. has
133. Is		143. strive
134. are		144. has
135. are		145. Every one

E. FAQs About Business English Review.

146. a	151. a
147. a	152. b
148. b	153. c
149. b	154. b
150. a	155. a

Chapter 7
A. Level 1 Preview

1. a		6. a
2. b		7. a
3. a		8. a
4. b		9. b
5. b		10. a

B. Adjectives and Adverbs.

11. b		18. a		25. a
12. b		19. a		26. a
13. b		20. b		27. a
14. b		21. b		28. b
15. a		22. b		29. b
16. b		23. b		30. b
17. b		24. b		

C.   Writing Exercise. Comparatives and Superlatives.

31. most current
32. easier
33. most (least) intellectual
34. better
35. more (less) quiet or quieter
36. least
37. more (less) professional
38. kinder
39. worst
40. worse

Level 2

A.   Level 2 Preview.

41. b
42. a
43. b
44. a
45. b
46. b
47. a
48. a
49. a
50. a

B.   Adjectives and Adverbs.

51. a
52. b
53. a
54. a
55. b
56. b
57. b
58. b
59. b
60. a
61. a
62. b
63. b
64. b
65. a
66. b
67. a
68. b
69. b
70. a

C.   Articles.

71. a
72. an
73. an
74. a
75. a
76. a
77. an
78. an
79. an
80. a
81. an
82. an
83. an
84. a
85. an

D.   Compound Adjectives.

86. b
87. b
88. b
89. a
90. a
91. a
92. b
93. b
94. b
95. b
96. b
97. b
98. a
99. b
100. a
101. b
102. b
103. a
104. b
105. b

E.   Independent Adjectives.

106. a
107. b
108. b
109. a
110. b

111. b
112. b
113. a
114. a
115. a

F.   Writing Exercise. Compound Adjectives.

Answers will vary.

116. The company merger will produce many long-term benefits.
117. He bought a first-class ticket to Barcelona.
118. She was offered a part-time position.
119. Our two-year-old equipment already needs upgrading.
120. This is a once-in-a-lifetime opportunity.
121. Please follow the month-by-month plan.
122. Only work-related expenses are reimbursed.
123. Their latest model represents state-the-art technology.
124. All of her certifications are up-to-date.
125. Our local hospital offers outstanding health care services.

Level 3

A.   Level 3 Preview.

126. b
127. b
128. b
129. a
130. a

131. b
132. b
133. a
134. b
135. b

B.   Adjectives and Adverbs.

136. a
137. b
138. b
139. a
140. a
141. b
142. a

143. b
144. a
145. b
146. a
147. b
148. b
149. a

150. b
151. b
152. a
153. b
154. a
155. a

C.   Writing Exercise. Commonly Confused Adjectives and Adverbs.

Answers will vary.

156. How much farther is the gas station?
157. She is returning to school to further her education.
158. In comparing e-books and traditional books, I prefer the latter.
159. Fewer accidents were reported for this holiday than for holidays in previous years.
160. Less preparation is needed for entry-level jobs.

D.   Review. Adjectives and Adverbs.

161.	a	166.	a
162.	a	167.	b
163.	b	168.	a
164.	a	169.	b
165.	b	170.	b

E.   FAQs About Business English Review.

171.	a	176.	a
172.	b	177.	b
173.	b	178.	b
174.	a	179.	a
175.	b	180.	a

Chapter 8
Level 1
A.   Level 1 Preview.

1.	b	6.	b
2.	b	7.	a
3.	b	8.	a
4.	b	9.	b
5.	a	10.	b

B.   Prepositions.

11.	b	21.	b
12.	b	22.	a
13.	a	23.	b
14.	b	24.	b
15.	a	25.	a
16.	b	26.	b
17.	b	27.	b
18.	b	28.	b
19.	a	29.	a
20.	a	30.	b

Level 2
A.   Level 2 Preview.

31.	b	36.	b
32.	b	37.	b
33.	b	38.	a
34.	a	39.	a
35.	b	40.	a

B.   Writing Exercise. Necessary and Unnecessary Prepositions.

41.   Where should I send the defective product?
42.   A new café is opening opposite the park.
43.   Special printing jobs must be done outside the office.
44.   Charles had a great respect for and interest in the stock market.
45.   Who can tell me what time the appointment is scheduled?
46.   What style of clothes is recommended for the formal dinner?
47.   Leah couldn't help laughing when Noah spilled his latte as he walked into the conference room.
48.   Where did the department head go?
49.   Lee Montgomery graduated from college with a degree in graphic design.
50.   What type of return policy does Zappos.com have?
51.   Please write her performance appraisal quickly.
52.   Our appreciation for and interest in the program remain strong.
53.   When did you graduate from college?
54.   Where will the product department meeting be held?
55.   I didn't mean to wake you.

C.   Prepositions.

56.	a	66.	a
57.	b	67.	a
58.	b	68.	a
59.	b	69.	b
60.	a	70.	b
61.	a	71.	b
62.	a	72.	b
63.	b	73.	a
64.	a	74.	b
65.	b	75.	a

D.   Writing Exercise.

76.   To whom did you send your résumé?
77.   Please locate the Google Docs folder in which you put the contract file.
78.   For what positions did you apply?
79.   We have a number of loyal members upon whom we can rely.
80.   From what company did you purchase these supplies?

Level 3

A.   Level 3 Preview.

81.	a	86.	b
82.	a	87.	a
83.	a	88.	b
84.	a	89.	b
85.	a	90.	a

B. Idiomatic Expressions.

91.	b	101.	a
92.	b	102.	c
93.	a	103.	a
94.	a	104.	b
95.	b	105.	a
96.	a	106.	a
97.	c	107.	b
98.	b	108.	a
99.	b	109.	b
100.	a	110.	a

C. Writing Exercise: Idiomatic Expressions.

111. Working at her computer, Christie was oblivious to the chaos around her.
112. Cary often finds it difficult to reconcile the company checkbook with the bank statement.
113. Kelly is reconciled to the fact that her sister will always earn more than she does.
114. I plan to apply to graduate schools.
115. The model we received is different from the model we ordered online.

D. FAQs About Business English Review.

116.	a	121.	c
117.	b	122.	a
118.	b	123.	b
119.	a	124.	b
120.	a	125.	b

Chapter 9
Level 1

A. Level 1 Preview.

1.	a	6.	a
2.	b	7.	c
3.	c	8.	b
4.	a	9.	b
5.	b	10.	a

B. Coordinating Conjunctions.

11.	b	16.	a
12.	a	17.	a
13.	a	18.	a
14.	b	19.	b
15.	a	20.	a

C. Conjunctive Adverbs.

21.	b	26.	a
22.	a	27.	a
23.	b	28.	a
24.	b	29.	a
25.	b	30.	b

D. Writing Exercise. Using Coordinating Conjunctions and Conjunctive Adverbs.

Answers will vary.

31. Cecilia studied hard for her accounting exam, and she earned the highest grade in the class.

32. The three documents most commonly stolen by identity thieves are driver's licenses, social security cards, and medical records.

33. She is considering a career in data analysis or in finance.

34. This year we hired only one new employee, but next year we hope to add several more.

35. We are convinced that Grant has been embezzling finds, yet we have not taken action.

36. Sales are increasing dramatically; consequently, we will hire three additional salespeople.

37. We think, consequently, that we will need three new company cars.

38. Take photos of our new product offerings; then post them on Facebook.

39. We have been using social media to connect with our customers; however, we are seeing little change in our market share.

40. We are not sure, however, that the candidate is qualified for the position.

Level 2

A. Level 2 Preview.

41.	b	46.	a
42.	b	47.	a
43.	a	48.	a
44.	b	49.	a
45.	b	50.	b

B. Relative Clauses.

51.	b	56.	c
52.	c	57.	b
53.	a	58.	a
54.	b	59.	a
55.	a	60.	a

C. **Conjunctions.**

Coordinating Conjunctions	Conjunctive Adverbs	Subordinating Conjunctions
and	however	if
but	moreover	although
yet	consequently	because
nor	thus	since
or	then	when

D. **Punctuating Sentences With Dependent and Relative Clauses.**

61.	a	71.	b
62.	b	72.	a
63.	b	73.	b
64.	a	74.	a
65.	a	75.	a
66.	b	76.	b
67.	a	77.	b
68.	a	78.	a
69.	b	79.	a
70.	a	80.	b

E. **Writing Exercise. Subordinating Conjunctions and Relative Pronouns.**
Answers will vary.
81. If you agree with me, please let our team know.
82. Please let our team know if you agree with me.
83. Because so many of our employees telecommute, we are purchasing additional wireless devices.
84. Reece Soltani plans to work for Kiva because she believes in its mission.
85. Although most people today own a smartphone, many complain that other smartphone users are rude.
86. After I complete my degree, I will look for a permanent job.
87. Taxpayers who donate to charity will get tax breaks.
88. Bob Mensch, who donated to charity, received a tax break.
89. The idea that was adopted came from a group of students.
90. LL Bean, which was started in a basement in Maine in 1911, finally expanded to other states staring in 2000.

Level 3
A. **Level 3 Preview.**

91.	b	96.	c
92.	b	97.	b
93.	a	98.	a
94.	a	99.	b
95.	a	100.	d

B.   Correlative Conjunctions.

101. a   106. b
102. a   107. b
103. b   108. a
104. b   109. b
105. a   110. b

C.   Writing Exercise. Coordinating and Correlative Conjunctions.

Answers will vary.

111. Stocks can be purchased either online or by phone.

112. Neither the staff nor the students were happy with the proposed reductions in class offerings.

113. The Small Business Administration not only provides training but also guarantees loans.

114. Because smartphone users are often guilty of rude behavior, may restaurants have imposed bans. *OR:* Smartphone users are often guilty of rude behavior; therefore, may restaurants have imposed bans.

115. Because old computer hardware creates hazardous dump sites, many communities offer e-waste recycling programs. *OR:* Old computer hardware creates hazardous dump sites; therefore, many communities offer e-waste recycling programs.

D.   Writing Exercise. Sentence Variety.

Answers will vary.

116. Melinda, who was recently hired as an application support engineer, will work for MathWorks, which is located in Natick, Massachusetts.

117. While teaching international business protocol and social etiquette to business professionals, Syndi Seid, who is a trainer and celebrity speaker, discovered that companies today look for men and women who possess social polish and confidence.

118. Japanese ranchers, who learned that cows respond to beeps, equipped their herds with pagers; consequently, these ranchers need fewer workers.

119. Before sitting down at their computers, skilled writers save time for themselves and for their readers by organizing their ideas into logical patterns.

120. Nancy Burnett, who is a single parent with merchandising experience, started a mall-based chain of stores that sell fashionable, durable children's clothing.

E.   FAQs About Business Review.

121. b   126. b
122. c   127. a
123. a   128. b
124. a   129. a
125. b   130. b

Chapter 10

Level 1

A. Level 1 Preview.
1. series
2. parenthetical
3. date
4. geographical items
5. appositive
6. C—essential appositive
7. time zone
8. direct address
9. C—not a parenthetical
10. address

B. Commas.
11. series
12. date, time zone
13. date
14. C—essential appositive, date
15. series
16. parenthetical
17. direct address
18. series
19. parenthetical
20. appositive
21. C—date
22. parenthetical
23. parenthetical
24. series
25. C—one-word appositives
26. address
27. parenthetical
28. C—essential appositive
29. appositive
30. time zone

C. Commas.
31. direct address, geographical item
32. date
33. parenthetical
34. parenthetical, series
35. series
36. appositive
37. C—one-word appositive
38. series
39. C—series with conjunctions joining all items
40. geographical item, date
41. series
42. appositive, time zone
43. address
44. parenthetical expression, geographical items
45. series
46. appositive
47. direct address, series
48. parenthetical
49. series
50. C—essential appositive

Level 2

A. Level 2 Preview.
51. introductory verbal phrase
52. introductory dependent clause, the adverb *too*
53. prepositional phrase
54. C—short prepositional phrase
55. independent clauses
56. C—terminal dependent clause
57. unnecessary terminal dependent clause
58. C—essential clause
59. nonessential clause
60. independent adjectives

B. Commas.

61. C—the adverb *too*
62. C—short prepositional phrase
63. independent clauses
64. nonessential clause
65. C—short prepositional phrase
66. independent adjectives
67. introductory verbal phrase
68. introductory dependent clause
69. introductory dependent clause
70. nonessential clause

71. C—essential clause
72. introductory dependent clause
73. C—terminal dependent clause
74. independent clauses
75. nonessential clause
76. prepositional phrase
77. C—short prepositional phrase
78. independent adjectives
79. nonessential clause
80. the adverb *too*

C. Commas.

81. unnecessary terminal dependent clause
82. introductory dependent clause
83. the adverb *too*
84. independent clauses
85. independent adjectives, unnecessary terminal dependent clause
86. nonessential clause
87. introductory verbal phrase
88. independent adjectives
89. prepositional phrase
90. nonessential clause

91. independent clauses
92. C—short prepositional phrase
93. introductory dependent clause
94. independent adjectives
95. introductory dependent clause
96. introductory dependent clause, independent adjectives
97. C—one independent clause
98. nonessential clause
99. independent clauses
100. nonessential clause, series

Level 3

A. Level 3 Preview.

101. short quotation
102. repeated words
103. omitted words
104. degree
105. adjacent numerals, geographical items

106. numeral
107. contrasting statement
108. short quotation
109. short prepositional phrase, omitted words
110. repeated words

B. Commas.

111. short quotation
112. C—page number
113. contrasting statement
114. short quotation
115. adjacent numerals, numeral
116. C—short prepositional phrase, policy number
117. professional designations
118. clarity
119. contrasting statement
120. omitted words
121. contrasting statement
122. short quotation
123. clarity
124. degrees
125. adjacent numerals, numeral
126. contrasting statement
127. numerals, omitted words
128. repeated words
129. short quotation
130. C—house number

C. Writing Exercise. Comma Rules.

Answers will vary.

131.	Series	Available entrees include prime rib, grilled chicken, and vegetarian pasta.
132.	Parenthetical	All entrees, by the way, include salad and dessert.
133.	Introductory phrase	To make the deadline, you must apply online.
134.	Independent clauses	Mike praised his iPad, but Lisa preferred her Samsung Galaxy Note.
135.	Contrasting statement	It was Marcus, not Ally, who knew how to get to the conference.

D. Review. Commas.

136. direct address
137. geographical item, time zone
138. address
139. date, nonessential clause
140. appositive, series
141. parenthetical expression, geographical item, date
142. nonessential clause, geographical item
143. essential clause, geographical item
144. prepositional phrase
145. introductory dependent clause
146. introductory dependent clause, series
147. introductory verbal phrase
148. C—one independent clause
149. clarity
150. repeated words
151. numeral, series
152. contrasting statement
153. short quotation
154. series
155. C–short prepositional phrase

E. FAQs About Business English Review.

156. b
157. c
158. a
159. b
160. a
161. b
162. a
163. a
164. b
165. a

Chapter 11

A. **Level 1 Preview.**

1.	work;	6.	C
2.	communication;	7.	States,
3.	coder;	8.	list;
4.	interactive;	9.	petroleum;
5.	high;	10.	consumption;

B. **Commas and Semicolons.**

11.	2	21.	1
12.	2	22.	1
13.	2	23.	1
14.	1	24.	2
15.	9	25.	C
16.	1	26.	8
17.	1	27.	3
18.	1	28.	3
19.	2	29.	3
20.	1	30.	5

Level 2

A. **Level 2 Preview.**

31.	Omit colon	36.	Omit colon
32.	C	37.	C
33.	following.	38.	Omit colon
34.	state:	39.	C
35.	said:	40.	C

B. **Commas and Colons.**

41.	C	51.	3
42.	1	52.	C
43.	1	53.	C
44.	2	54.	C
45.	1	55.	C
46.	1	56.	1
47.	1	57.	1
48.	1	58.	1
49.	2	59.	1
50.	6	60.	1

C. **Writing exercise. Semicolons and Colons.**

61. Texting is used extensively in business today; therefore, the messages I send must be professional.

62. At work I use texting for business purposes only; at home I use it to write to my family and friends.

63. I would like to travel to Shanghai, China; Athens, Greece, Budapest, Hungary; and Bangkok, Thailand.

64. Good e-mail messages should feature the following: clarity, conciseness, and correct form.

65. I have one goal for taking this course: I want to improve my professional writing skills.

Level 3
A. Level 3 Preview.

66.	C	71.	C
67.	C	72.	C
68.	C	73.	1
69.	C	74.	C
70.	2	75.	C

B. Commas, Semicolons, and Colons.

76.	4	81.	5
77.	1	82.	2
78.	1	83.	2
79.	4	84.	8
80.	2	85.	1

C. FAQs About Business English Review.

86.	b	91.	a
87.	a	92.	b
88.	a	93.	a
89.	a	94.	a
90.	a	95.	b

Chapter 12
Level 1
A. Level 1 Review.

1.	.	6.	!
2.	!	7.	.
3.	?	8.	?
4.	?	9.	.
5.	.	10.	C

B. Periods, Question Marks, and Exclamation Marks.

11.	b	16.	a
12.	c	17.	b
13.	a	18.	b
14.	c	19.	b
15.	a	20.	a

C. Punctuation.

21.	c		26.	a
22.	b		27.	c
23.	a		28.	b
24.	c		29.	a
25.	c		30.	a

Level 2

A. Level 2 Preview.

31.	b		36.	c
32.	a		37.	a
33.	b		38.	a
34.	b		39.	b
35.	a		40.	c

B. Hyphenation.

41.	b		51.	a
42.	a		52.	b
43.	b		53.	b
44.	a		54.	a
45.	a		55.	b
46.	a		56.	b
47.	b		57.	b
48.	a		58.	a
49.	a		59.	a
50.	a		60.	b

C. Dashes and Parentheses.

61.	2		66.	1
62.	1		67.	2
63.	1		68.	2
64.	2		69.	2
65.	2		70.	2

D. Writing Exercise. Commas, Dashes, and Parentheses.

71. Ten-year-old Cory Nieves, the youngest CEO in the United States, founded Mr. Cory's Cookies when he was just five years old.

72. Ten-year-old Cory Nieves (the youngest CEO in the United States) founded Mr. Cory's Cookies when he was just five years old.

73. Ten-year-old Cory Nieves—the youngest CEO in the United States—founded Mr. Cory's Cookies when he was just five years old.

Level 3

A.   Level 3 Preview.

74.	F	79.	T
75.	T	80.	T
76.	F	81.	T
77.	T	82.	F
78.	T	83.	T

B.   Punctuation Sentences.

84.   The graduating class of '07 held its ten-year reunion on a cruise ship.

85.   Four fast-food restaurants (Taco Bell, Krispy Kreme, Burger King, and McDonald's) are extremely popular in India.

86.   China's favorite America brands include General Motors, Apple, Nike, and Starbucks.

87.   Debbi Fields, founder of Mrs. Fields Cookies, said, "You do not have to be superhuman to do what you believe in."

88.   "Whether you think you can or think you can't," said Henry Ford, "you're right."

89.   The word *tethering* is a technology term that means "to share the Internet connection of an Internet-capable smartphone or tablet computer with other devices."

90.   A chapter titled "Magic Words and Dangerous Descriptors" appears in the book *Zillow Talk: The New Rules of Real Estate.*

91.   Did the Roman philosopher Seneca really say, "Luck is what happens when preparation meets opportunity"?

92.   In his speech the software billionaire said, "Our goal is to link the world irregardless [*sic*] of national boundaries and restrictions."

93.   Oprah Winfrey said that the best jobs are those we'd do even if we didn't get paid.

94.   Garth says he plans to do a lot of "chillaxing" during his vacation.

95.   The postal worker said, "Shall I stamp your package *Fragile*?"

96.   Did you see the article titled "Hacking the Hackers: Why Companies Want to Strike Back" in *BusinessWeek*?

97.   The French expression *répondez s'il vous plaît* means "respond if you please."

98.   Many people are surprised to learn that Bruno Mars is only 5'5" because he has such stage presence.

99.   "The human race has only one really effective weapon," said Mark Twain, "and that is laughter."

100.   Three of the top contractors—Kayler Construction, The Shaw Group, and Flatiron Construction Corporation—submitted bids.

101.   In *Forbes* I saw an article titled "App. Battle: Who Does Food Delivery Best?"

102.   Albert Einstein once said that only two things (the universe and human stupidity) are infinite.

103.   Albert Einstein once said that only two things—the universe and human stupidity—are infinite.

C: **Writing Exercise. Using Punctuation Marks.**
Answers will vary.

D. **FAQs About Business English Review.**

104.	b	109.	a
105.	a	110.	c
106.	a	111.	a
107.	b	112.	b
108.	b	113.	a

Chapter 13

Level 1

A. **Level 1 Preview.**

1.	9	6.	5
2.	8	7.	4
3.	4	8.	4
4.	8	9.	1
5.	2	10.	7

B. **Capitalization.**

11.	5	21.	7
12.	4	22.	8
13.	2	23.	3
14.	4	24.	6
15.	7	25.	8
16.	3	26.	3
17.	3	27.	3
18.	4	28.	7
19.	8	29.	5
20.	6	30.	7

Level 2

A. **Level 2 Preview.**

31.	6	36.	5
32.	2	37.	5
33.	4	38.	3
34.	4	39.	4
35.	4	40.	5

B. Capitalization.

41.	4	51.	3
42.	4	52.	5
43.	6	53.	4
44.	2	54.	3
45.	6	55.	4
46.	12	56.	4
47.	1	57.	5
48.	5	58.	3
49.	3	59.	3
50.	4	60.	4

Level 3

A. Level 3 Preview.

61.	4	66.	6
62.	1	67.	3
63.	3	68.	5
64.	4	69.	4
65.	3	70.	1

B. Capitalization.

71.	5	76.	6
72.	2	77.	4
73.	2	78.	7
74.	1	79.	3
75.	5	80.	7

C. Review. Capitalization.

81.	a	91.	b
82.	b	92.	a
83.	b	93.	a
84.	a	94.	b
85.	a	95.	a
86.	b	96.	b
87.	b	97.	b
88.	a	98.	b
89.	a	99.	a
90.	b	100.	b

D. Writing Exercise. Using Capitalization.
Answers will vary.

E.   FAQs About Business English Review.

101. b	106. b
102. b	107 b
103. a	108 a
104. b	109 a
105. a	110. b

Chapter 14
Level 1
A.   Level 1 Preview.

1. b	6. b
2. c	7. a
3. a	8. a
4. b	9. b
5. b	10. b

B.   Number Expression.

11. 16 new job listings	26. 1,319 people visited
12. C	27. C
13. charged 2 cents per business card	28. the address is One Hampton Square
14. received nine text messages	29. payroll expense of $2,500
15. on December 19	30. at 18:00
16. located on Third Avenue	31. on 15 April 2018
17. charges of $3.68, $.79, and $40	32. located at 2742 Eighth Street
18. on the 15th of December	33. at 6:30 p.m.
19. meeting at 8 a.m.	34. costs $25
20. arrived at 10 p.m.	35. for $100
21. a total of 57 orders	36. costs exactly 90 cents
22. on October 31	37. at 18307 11th Street
23. C	38. call (800) 598-3459
24. opens at 8:30 a.m.	39. C
25. Twenty-seven interviewees	40. hired two new employees

C.   Writing Exercise. Number Expression.

41. A total of 783 data breaches were reported in the United States in one year alone.
42. Please call me at (925) 685-1230, Ext. 2306.
43. On November 15 Ivan submitted the following petty cash disbursements: $2.80, $.95, $5, and $.25.
44. Erika Rothschild moved from 1716 Sunset Drive to One Bellingham Court.
45. Nineteen people plan to run for two open town council positions.
46. On the 18th of August, I sent you three e-mail messages about our upcoming ethics training.
47. Although McDonald's advertised a sandwich that cost only 99 cents, most customers found that lunch cost between $3 and $3.99.
48. Regular work breaks are scheduled at 10 a.m. and again at 3:30 p.m.

49. We want to continue operations through the 30th, but we may be forced to close by the 22nd.

50. Monaco has a population of 35,000 making it one of the smallest countries in the world.

Level 2

A. Level 2 Preview.

51.	b	56.	a
52.	b	57.	b
53.	b	58.	b
54.	a	59.	a
55.	b	60.	a

B. Number Expression.

61.	35,000, 10	71.	82
62.	Number 3, 45	72.	44, 2, $576 billion
63.	3, 4, 8	73.	90
64.	five 12-month	74.	800,000
65.	16	75.	2
66.	one million, 1.4 billion	76.	twenty-four
67.	numbers	77.	2 years 6 months
68.	8400	78.	24, 200, 23
69.	2.44 billion	79.	seven, $63 million
70.	10, 8	80.	40 million

C. Number Expression.

81.	sold for $8.9 million	90.	Highway 6
82.	104 6-page essays	91.	you are No. 25
83.	a law that is a 1 year 2 months and 5 days old	92.	63 job applicants
84.	nine offices with 11 computers and 15 desks	93.	C or about 200 applications
85.	three 75-pound Irish setters	94.	4.4 million people
86.	loan period of 90 days	95.	Section 3.2
87.	Joan Brault, 79, and Frank Brault, 77	96.	nine 3-bedroom apartments
88.	Account No. 362486012	97.	warranty period of 2 years (business term)
89.	$4.9 billion	98.	C
		99.	selected Nos. 305 and 409
		100.	took out a 9-month CD (business term)

Level 3

A.   Level 3 Preview.

101. a	106. a
102. a	107. a
103. b	108. a
104. a	109. b
105. a	110. a

B.   Writing Exercise. Using Numbers.

111. Formula Rossa, which is the world's fastest roller coaster, reaches speeds of 150 miles per hour in just 4.9 seconds.

112. When the ride first opened on November 4, 2010, nearly one third of the visitors to Ferrari World in Abu Dhabi lined up for a high-speed joyride on four 16-passenger rail cars.

113. Engineers with Intamin used precise instruments to ensure that Formula Rossa's 1.4 miles of steel track were within .05 inches of specifications.

114. To ride Formula Rossa, you must be at least 55 inches but less than 6 feet 5 inches tall.

115. A ride on the Formula Rossa roller coaster, which lasts 1 minute 32 seconds and climbs to 174 feet, lets riders experience the feeling of traveling at 1.7 g-forces.

116. Located in Abu Dhabi, Ferrari World is situated under a 2,152,782-square-foot roof, making it the largest indoor amusement park in the world.

117. Washington, DC, occupies 68.3 square miles; and its population is about 659,000.

118. Although Washington, DC, has a population of 658,893, its population during the week grows to approximately one million because of commuters.

119. African Americans make up approximately 49.5 percent of the population in Washington, DC.

120. Even though one half of Washington, DC, residents have at least a four-year college degree, one third of all residents are functionally illiterate.

C.   Writing Exercise. Using Numbers

Answers will vary.

D.   FAQs About Business English Review.

121. c	126. a
122. a	127. a
123. b	128. b
124. a	129. a
125. b	130. b